THE

BIBLE RECAP

JOURNAL

YOUR DAILY COMPANION TO
THE ENTIRE BIBLE

TARA-LEIGH COBBLE

BETHANYHOUSE
a division of Baker Publishing Group
Minneapolis, Minnesota

Published by Bethany House Publishers
11400 Hampshire Avenue South
Minneapolis, Minnesota 55438
www.bethanyhouse.com

Bethany House Publishers is a division of
Baker Publishing Group, Grand Rapids, Michigan

Printed in the United States of America

ISBN 978-0-7642-4031-7

Cover design by Rob Williams, InsideOut Creative Arts, Inc.

The Bible Recap logo design by Landon Wade

The author is represented by Alive Literary Agency, www.aliveliterary.com.

Baker Publishing Group publications use paper produced from sustainable forestry practices and post-consumer waste whenever possible.

22   23   24   25   26   27   7   6   5   4   3   2

How to Use This Journal and Other Tools

First, please visit **thebiblerecap.com/start**. It will tell you all you need to know to join our reading plan and podcast. Then, we recommend doing the following steps each day, in this order:

1. Do your daily Bible reading according to The Bible Recap reading plan you've chosen: whole Bible (Old Testament and New Testament) or New Testament only.

2. Use this journal during your reading. For each day, you'll find three writing prompts, including space to record your "God Shot"—where you see God's attributes on display in that day's reading. It's called a God Shot because it's a snapshot of God's character. He's on every page of Scripture, so keep your eyes peeled for things that reveal Him to you—what He says and does, what He loves and hates, and what motivates Him to do what He does.

3. Use *The Bible Recap Study Guide* after (or during) each day's reading. There's room underneath the questions where you can write your answers in the guide itself, which is sold separately.

4. Listen to the corresponding podcast episode or read the entry in *The Bible Recap* book for more information, insights, and answers.

5. And lastly, use the *Weekly Discussion Guide*, available at thebiblerecap.com, in group conversations about that week's reading plan. Since these questions are intended for group discussion, we did not aim to create space for answering in the weekly guide itself.

This journal is intended to be self-guided, while the daily and weekly guides offer a higher level of challenge and connection. You don't have to have both guides (*The Bible Recap Study Guide* and the *Weekly Discussion Guide*), but we created them with the intention of complementing each other.

Before you read God's Word each day, seek His help with these five prayers:

1. Give me wisdom, knowledge, and understanding.
2. Let any knowledge I gain serve to help me love You and others more, and not puff me up.
3. Help me see something new about You I've never seen before.
4. Correct any lies I believe about You or anything I misunderstand.
5. Direct my steps according to Your Word.

GENESIS 1–3

Things I loved / learned / noticed:

How God had people Guard
the tree so they couldn't
eat it any more!

Questions / things I want to research:

More on Adam & Eve's story

God Shot:

"The enemy's attempts to thwart the
Bloodline of Christ don't Prevail.
"He's at work in all things to Restore
Fallen humanity in Relationship with
Himself!

By telling us His name, God is showing us right out of the
gate that He wants to be personal with His creation.

GENESIS 4–7

Things I loved / learned / noticed:

_____

_____

_____

_____

Questions / things I want to research:

_____

_____

_____

_____

God Shot:

_____

_____

_____

_____

Nothing can thwart God's will. Nothing can keep
Him from His plan to rescue His people.

GENESIS 8–11

Things I loved / learned / noticed:

_____

_____

_____

_____

Questions / things I want to research:

_____

_____

_____

_____

God Shot:

_____

_____

_____

_____

Pray: Father, I'm so grateful You adopted me into Your family.
You pursued and redeemed me. May I never take Your mercy for granted.

DAY 4

JOB 1–5

Things I loved / learned / noticed:

_____

_____

_____

_____

Questions / things I want to research:

_____

_____

_____

_____

God Shot:

_____

_____

_____

_____

"In all this Job did not sin
or charge God with wrong."—Job 1:22

JOB 6–9

Things I loved / learned / noticed:

_____

_____

_____

_____

Questions / things I want to research:

_____

_____

_____

_____

God Shot:

_____

_____

_____

_____

Mercy is when you don't get what you deserve.
Grace is when you *get* what you *don't* deserve.

DAY 6

JOB 10–13

Things I loved / learned / noticed:

_____

_____

_____

_____

Questions / things I want to research:

_____

_____

_____

_____

God Shot:

_____

_____

_____

_____

Pray: God, You're my redeemer and my hope. I deserved hell and
death, but You saved me. Help me to humbly live this truth every day.

JOB 14–16

Things I loved / learned / noticed:

_____

_____

_____

_____

Questions / things I want to research:

_____

_____

_____

_____

God Shot:

_____

_____

_____

_____

God is sovereign over our life-span. This should serve
as a great comfort, because He is trustworthy!

JOB 17–20

Things I loved / learned / noticed:

_____

_____

_____

_____

Questions / things I want to research:

_____

_____

_____

_____

God Shot:

_____

_____

_____

_____

"I know that my Redeemer lives, and at the last
he will stand upon the earth."—Job 19:25

JOB 21–23

Things I loved / learned / noticed:

_____

_____

_____

_____

Questions / things I want to research:

_____

_____

_____

_____

God Shot:

_____

_____

_____

_____

In the grand scheme of things, don't we *want* God to call us
out of our sin? It's His kindness that prompts us to repent.

JOB 24–28

Things I loved / learned / noticed:

_____

_____

_____

_____

Questions / things I want to research:

_____

_____

_____

_____

God Shot:

_____

_____

_____

_____

Pray: Thank You, God, that You're the source of all wisdom.
May I always remember that the fear of the Lord is wisdom
and that turning away from evil displays understanding.

JOB 29–31

Things I loved / learned / noticed:

_____

_____

_____

_____

Questions / things I want to research:

_____

_____

_____

_____

God Shot:

_____

_____

_____

_____

You can only trust someone you know, and you can only
know someone you spend time with. May our knowledge
of God and our trust of God always be increasing.

JOB 32–34

Things I loved / learned / noticed:

_____

_____

_____

_____

Questions / things I want to research:

_____

_____

_____

_____

God Shot:

_____

_____

_____

_____

"God certainly will not do wickedly, and the Almighty
will not pervert justice."—Job 34:12

JOB 35–37

Things I loved / learned / noticed:

_____

_____

_____

_____

Questions / things I want to research:

_____

_____

_____

_____

God Shot:

_____

_____

_____

_____

We can rest knowing God's working
in all things for His glory and our joy.

JOB 38–39

Things I loved / learned / noticed:

_____

_____

_____

_____

Questions / things I want to research:

_____

_____

_____

_____

God Shot:

_____

_____

_____

_____

God's not threatened by our questions, but He's also not
required to give us any of the answers we're seeking.

JOB 40–42

Things I loved / learned / noticed:

_____

_____

_____

_____

Questions / things I want to research:

_____

_____

_____

_____

God Shot:

_____

_____

_____

_____

Pray: God, when You feel distant, remind me in a strong way how near
You really are. Thank You for Your unmatched patience and love.

GENESIS 12–15

Things I loved / learned / noticed:

_____

_____

_____

_____

Questions / things I want to research:

_____

_____

_____

_____

God Shot:

_____

_____

_____

_____

"And [Abram] believed the LORD, and he counted
it to him as righteousness."—Genesis 15:6

GENESIS 16–18

Things I loved / learned / noticed:

_____

_____

_____

_____

Questions / things I want to research:

_____

_____

_____

_____

God Shot:

_____

_____

_____

_____

Pray: O Lord, I praise You for being El Roi, the God who sees me.
Keep me from taking matters into my own hands—I trust You.

GENESIS 19–21

Things I loved / learned / noticed:

_____

_____

_____

_____

Questions / things I want to research:

_____

_____

_____

_____

God Shot:

_____

_____

_____

_____

Not only does God forgive, but He wants to display His heart
of forgiveness to a broken world through us, His people.

GENESIS 22–24

Things I loved / learned / noticed:

_____

_____

_____

_____

Questions / things I want to research:

_____

_____

_____

_____

God Shot:

_____

_____

_____

_____

It's not the size of our faith that makes
things happen—it's the plan of our God.

DATE

GENESIS 25–26

Things I loved / learned / noticed:

_____

_____

_____

_____

Questions / things I want to research:

_____

_____

_____

_____

God Shot:

_____

_____

_____

_____

The more we're aware of our need for God, the more
our hearts remember that He's where the joy is!

GENESIS 27–29

Things I loved / learned / noticed:

Questions / things I want to research:

God Shot:

GENESIS 30–31

Things I loved / learned / noticed:

_____

_____

_____

_____

Questions / things I want to research:

_____

_____

_____

_____

God Shot:

_____

_____

_____

_____

Does God hate sin and injustice and ingratitude? Absolutely.
But remember, we've been adopted by a kind Father.

GENESIS 32–34

Things I loved / learned / noticed:

_____

_____

_____

_____

Questions / things I want to research:

_____

_____

_____

_____

God Shot:

_____

_____

_____

_____

God changes hearts, and difficult circumstances
are often His tool of choice.

GENESIS 35–37

Things I loved / learned / noticed:

_____

_____

_____

_____

Questions / things I want to research:

_____

_____

_____

_____

God Shot:

_____

_____

_____

_____

GENESIS 38–40

Things I loved / learned / noticed:

Questions / things I want to research:

God Shot:

"The Lord was with Joseph and showed him steadfast love and gave him favor in the sight of the keeper of the prison."—Genesis 39:21

GENESIS 41–42

Things I loved / learned / noticed:

_____

_____

_____

_____

Questions / things I want to research:

_____

_____

_____

_____

God Shot:

_____

_____

_____

_____

Even in the pit and the prison, Joseph knew that a very real
sense of joy was possible, because God was with him.

GENESIS 43–45

Things I loved / learned / noticed:

Questions / things I want to research:

God Shot:

GENESIS 46–47

Things I loved / learned / noticed:

_____

_____

_____

_____

Questions / things I want to research:

_____

_____

_____

_____

God Shot:

_____

_____

_____

_____

GENESIS 48–50

Things I loved / learned / noticed:

_____

_____

_____

_____

Questions / things I want to research:

_____

_____

_____

God Shot:

_____

_____

_____

_____

"As for you, you meant evil against me, but God
meant it for good."—Genesis 50:20

EXODUS 1–3

Things I loved / learned / noticed:

_____

_____

_____

_____

Questions / things I want to research:

_____

_____

_____

_____

God Shot:

_____

_____

_____

_____

God uses broken people. He seems to
specialize in using the unlikely.

EXODUS 4–6

Things I loved / learned / noticed:

_____

_____

_____

_____

Questions / things I want to research:

_____

_____

_____

_____

God Shot:

_____

_____

_____

_____

Pray: Father, help me to keep my eyes on You. When life is hard,
when hope is waning, lift me with Your love and power.

EXODUS 7–9

Things I loved / learned / noticed:

_____

_____

_____

_____

Questions / things I want to research:

_____

_____

_____

_____

God Shot:

_____

_____

_____

_____

The enemy loves to counterfeit God's work, but
the enemy can't stop God's work.

EXODUS 10–12

Things I loved / learned / noticed:

_____

_____

_____

_____

Questions / things I want to research:

_____

_____

_____

_____

God Shot:

_____

_____

_____

_____

We don't need God to help us; we need
His utter and complete rescue.

DAY 34

EXODUS 13–15

Things I loved / learned / noticed:

Questions / things I want to research:

God Shot:

"The Lord is my strength and my song,
and he has become my salvation."—Exodus 15:2

EXODUS 16–18

Things I loved / learned / noticed:

Questions / things I want to research:

God Shot:

God knows our human nature longs to earn things, to feel accomplished. But the very nature of His relationship with us is that we're the recipients, not the earners, not the doers.

EXODUS 19–21

Things I loved / learned / noticed:

_____

_____

_____

_____

Questions / things I want to research:

_____

_____

_____

_____

God Shot:

_____

_____

_____

_____

Pray: I need You, God. You give me joy and You
protect me. May I always be in awe of You.

EXODUS 22–24

Things I loved / learned / noticed:

_____

_____

_____

_____

Questions / things I want to research:

_____

_____

_____

_____

God Shot:

_____

_____

_____

_____

God pursues His enemies
and turns them into His family.

EXODUS 25–27

Things I loved / learned / noticed:

_____

_____

_____

_____

Questions / things I want to research:

_____

_____

_____

_____

God Shot:

_____

_____

_____

_____

Our God is a God of detail.

EXODUS 28–29

Things I loved / learned / noticed:

Questions / things I want to research:

God Shot:

EXODUS 30–32

Things I loved / learned / noticed:

_____
_____
_____
_____

Questions / things I want to research:

_____
_____
_____
_____

God Shot:

_____
_____
_____
_____

Whatever God requires of us,
He equips us for.

EXODUS 33–35

Things I loved / learned / noticed:

Questions / things I want to research:

God Shot:

"The Lord, a God merciful and gracious, slow to anger, and abounding in steadfast love and faithfulness."—Exodus 34:6

EXODUS 36–38

Things I loved / learned / noticed:

_____

_____

_____

_____

Questions / things I want to research:

_____

_____

_____

_____

God Shot:

_____

_____

_____

_____

Pray: Father, I praise You that You're always at work,
always near. Help me to trust this truth when I don't
understand what loved ones or I am going through.

EXODUS 39–40

Things I loved / learned / noticed:

Questions / things I want to research:

God Shot:

The glory of the Lord filled the tabernacle.
Every square inch, it seems.
His glory is dense, and His presence is undeniable.

DATE

LEVITICUS 1–4

Things I loved / learned / noticed:

_____

_____

_____

_____

Questions / things I want to research:

_____

_____

_____

_____

God Shot:

_____

_____

_____

_____

Sin is sin
regardless of motive.

LEVITICUS 5–7

Things I loved / learned / noticed:

_____

_____

_____

_____

Questions / things I want to research:

_____

_____

_____

_____

God Shot:

_____

_____

_____

_____

From the beginning of humanity, sinners have been running from God,
trying to hide, and He's been pursuing us, telling us to draw near.

DATE

LEVITICUS 8–10

Things I loved / learned / noticed:

_____

_____

_____

_____

Questions / things I want to research:

_____

_____

_____

_____

God Shot:

_____

_____

_____

_____

Pray: God, I'm so grateful for what I'm learning through
Your Word. By spending time with You, I know more
and more that You're where the joy is!

LEVITICUS 11–13

Things I loved / learned / noticed:

_____

_____

_____

_____

Questions / things I want to research:

_____

_____

_____

_____

God Shot:

_____

_____

_____

_____

"I am the Lord your God.
Consecrate yourselves therefore, and be holy,
for I am holy."—Leviticus 11:44

DAY 48

LEVITICUS 14–15

Things I loved / learned / noticed:

Questions / things I want to research:

God Shot:

God the Judge declares us righteous, even though we're
sinners, because of what Christ did on our behalf.

LEVITICUS 16–18

Things I loved / learned / noticed:

_____

_____

_____

_____

Questions / things I want to research:

_____

_____

_____

_____

God Shot:

_____

_____

_____

_____

Pray: Father, help me to live righteously. I confess that I'm
sinful. Thank You for Jesus who paid the price for my sins.

DAY 50

LEVITICUS 19–21

Things I loved / learned / noticed:

_____

_____

_____

_____

Questions / things I want to research:

_____

_____

_____

_____

God Shot:

_____

_____

_____

_____

There's a great distance between God's holiness and our
uncleanness, but take heart—His Spirit sanctifies us!

LEVITICUS 22–23

Things I loved / learned / noticed:

Questions / things I want to research:

God Shot:

How beautiful is it that God still wants to be
near us even though we're imperfect?

LEVITICUS 24–25

Things I loved / learned / noticed:

_____

_____

_____

_____

Questions / things I want to research:

_____

_____

_____

_____

God Shot:

_____

_____

_____

_____

Pray: O God, I praise You for Your generous love.
Everything I have is from Your hand.
Show me today and every day how I can bless others.

LEVITICUS 26–27

Things I loved / learned / noticed:

_____

_____

_____

_____

Questions / things I want to research:

_____

_____

_____

_____

God Shot:

_____

_____

_____

_____

"I . . . brought you out of the land of Egypt, that you should
not be their slaves. And I have broken the bars of your
yoke and made you walk erect."—Leviticus 26:13

DATE

NUMBERS 1–2

Things I loved / learned / noticed:

_____

_____

_____

_____

Questions / things I want to research:

_____

_____

_____

_____

God Shot:

_____

_____

_____

_____

Pray: God, I praise You for Your good plan for my life. You
know what's best for me. Your promises can be trusted.

NUMBERS 3–4

Things I loved / learned / noticed:

Questions / things I want to research:

God Shot:

Everyone who serves the church has a vital role, appointed
by God for the service and upbuilding of His people.

NUMBERS 5–6

Things I loved / learned / noticed:

_____

_____

_____

_____

Questions / things I want to research:

_____

_____

_____

_____

God Shot:

_____

_____

_____

_____

"The Lord bless you and keep you; the Lord make his face
to shine upon you and be gracious to you; the Lord lift up his
countenance upon you and give you peace."—Numbers 6:24–26

NUMBERS 7

Things I loved / learned / noticed:

_____

_____

_____

_____

Questions / things I want to research:

_____

_____

_____

_____

God Shot:

_____

_____

_____

_____

God is efficient.
He uses the gift of one
to bless the whole.

NUMBERS 8–10

Things I loved / learned / noticed:

_____

_____

_____

_____

Questions / things I want to research:

_____

_____

_____

_____

God Shot:

_____

_____

_____

_____

Pray: I don't deserve it, Lord, but thank You for setting me apart.
Help me to know how dependent I am on You. Keep me close.

NUMBERS 11–13

Things I loved / learned / noticed:

Questions / things I want to research:

God Shot:

DAY 60

DATE

NUMBERS 14–15; PSALM 90

Things I loved / learned / noticed:

Questions / things I want to research:

God Shot:

The Sabbath reminds us who God is; it's an act of trust.

NUMBERS 16–17

Things I loved / learned / noticed:

_____

_____

_____

_____

Questions / things I want to research:

_____

_____

_____

_____

God Shot:

_____

_____

_____

_____

DATE

NUMBERS 18–20

Things I loved / learned / noticed:

_____

_____

_____

_____

Questions / things I want to research:

_____

_____

_____

_____

God Shot:

_____

_____

_____

_____

NUMBERS 21–22

Things I loved / learned / noticed:

_____

_____

_____

_____

Questions / things I want to research:

_____

_____

_____

_____

God Shot:

_____

_____

_____

_____

God has power over what we see;
He can hide and reveal things at will.

NUMBERS 23–25

Things I loved / learned / noticed:

_____

_____

_____

_____

Questions / things I want to research:

_____

_____

_____

_____

God Shot:

_____

_____

_____

_____

"God is not man, that he should lie, or a son of man,
that he should change his mind."—Numbers 23:19

NUMBERS 26–27

Things I loved / learned / noticed:

Questions / things I want to research:

God Shot:

NUMBERS 28–30

Things I loved / learned / noticed:

Questions / things I want to research:

God Shot:

NUMBERS 31–32

Things I loved / learned / noticed:

_____

_____

_____

_____

Questions / things I want to research:

_____

_____

_____

_____

God Shot:

_____

_____

_____

_____

"Be killing sin, or it will be killing you."
—John Owen

DATE

NUMBERS 33–34

Things I loved / learned / noticed:

_____

_____

_____

_____

Questions / things I want to research:

_____

_____

_____

_____

God Shot:

_____

_____

_____

_____

Pray: O God, You're the King of kings and Lord of lords.
You alone deserve our affection and attention.

NUMBERS 35–36

Things I loved / learned / noticed:

Questions / things I want to research:

God Shot:

May each new need in our lives remind us that our ultimate,
constant need is for God and His wisdom and guidance.

DEUTERONOMY 1–2

Things I loved / learned / noticed:

_____

_____

_____

_____

Questions / things I want to research:

_____

_____

_____

_____

God Shot:

_____

_____

_____

_____

God is generous,
even to those who aren't His children!

DEUTERONOMY 3–4

Things I loved / learned / noticed:

_____

_____

_____

_____

Questions / things I want to research:

_____

_____

_____

_____

God Shot:

_____

_____

_____

_____

"Keep your soul diligently, lest you forget the things that your eyes have seen, and lest they depart from your heart."—Deuteronomy 4:9

DAY 72

DEUTERONOMY 5–7

Things I loved / learned / noticed:

_____

_____

_____

_____

Questions / things I want to research:

_____

_____

_____

_____

God Shot:

_____

_____

_____

_____

"Love the LORD your God with all your heart and with all your soul and with all your might."—Deuteronomy 6:5

DEUTERONOMY 8–10

Things I loved / learned / noticed:

Questions / things I want to research:

God Shot:

We can't earn God's blessings; they're a gift—
freely given to the undeserving.

DEUTERONOMY 11–13

Things I loved / learned / noticed:

_____

_____

_____

_____

Questions / things I want to research:

_____

_____

_____

_____

God Shot:

_____

_____

_____

_____

Pray: Help me to obey Your commands, God. They reveal
how much You love me and want to protect me.

DEUTERONOMY 14–16

Things I loved / learned / noticed:

_____

_____

_____

_____

Questions / things I want to research:

_____

_____

_____

_____

God Shot:

_____

_____

_____

_____

God has always been after our hearts,
not just our obedience.

DEUTERONOMY 17–20

Things I loved / learned / noticed:

_____

_____

_____

_____

Questions / things I want to research:

_____

_____

_____

_____

God Shot:

_____

_____

_____

_____

DEUTERONOMY 21–23

Things I loved / learned / noticed:

_____

_____

_____

Questions / things I want to research:

_____

_____

_____

God Shot:

_____

_____

_____

The God who turns our curse to a blessing is
a God worth worshipping forever.

DEUTERONOMY 24–27

Things I loved / learned / noticed:

_____

_____

_____

_____

Questions / things I want to research:

_____

_____

_____

_____

God Shot:

_____

_____

_____

_____

How beautiful to be treasured, possessed, and
loved infinitely by an infinitely lovable God.

DEUTERONOMY 28–29

Things I loved / learned / noticed:

_____

_____

_____

_____

Questions / things I want to research:

_____

_____

_____

_____

God Shot:

_____

_____

_____

_____

Pray: Father, please keep me from trusting myself too much.
I need Your wisdom. You know what's best for me.

DEUTERONOMY 30–31

Things I loved / learned / noticed:

_____

_____

_____

_____

Questions / things I want to research:

_____

_____

_____

_____

God Shot:

_____

_____

_____

_____

"It is the LORD who goes before you. He will
be with you."—Deuteronomy 31:8

DEUTERONOMY 32–34; PSALM 91

Things I loved / learned / noticed:

_____
_____
_____
_____

Questions / things I want to research:

_____
_____
_____
_____

God Shot:

_____
_____
_____
_____

As you read His Word, your heart is being
knit to Him in deeper ways.

JOSHUA 1–4

Things I loved / learned / noticed:

_____

_____

_____

_____

Questions / things I want to research:

_____

_____

_____

_____

God Shot:

_____

_____

_____

_____

God never asks us to do things on our own;
His nearness is what equips us to obey.

JOSHUA 5–8

Things I loved / learned / noticed:

Questions / things I want to research:

God Shot:

DATE

JOSHUA 9–11

Things I loved / learned / noticed:

_____

_____

_____

_____

Questions / things I want to research:

_____

_____

_____

_____

God Shot:

_____

_____

_____

_____

JOSHUA 12–15

Things I loved / learned / noticed:

_____

_____

_____

_____

Questions / things I want to research:

_____

_____

_____

_____

God Shot:

_____

_____

_____

_____

Even in failure, trust can grow, faith can be
strengthened, and joy can be found.

JOSHUA 16–18

Things I loved / learned / noticed:

_____

_____

_____

Questions / things I want to research:

_____

_____

_____

_____

God Shot:

_____

_____

_____

_____

JOSHUA 19–21

Things I loved / learned / noticed:

_____

_____

_____

_____

Questions / things I want to research:

_____

_____

_____

_____

God Shot:

_____

_____

_____

_____

"Not one word of all the good promises that the Lord had made to the house of Israel had failed; all came to pass."—Joshua 21:45

JOSHUA 22–24

Things I loved / learned / noticed:

_____

_____

_____

_____

Questions / things I want to research:

_____

_____

_____

_____

God Shot:

_____

_____

_____

_____

God is failproof,
and He's where the joy is!

JUDGES 1–2

Things I loved / learned / noticed:

Questions / things I want to research:

God Shot:

Nothing changes unless hearts change. God's love
for us prompts our hearts to love Him back.

JUDGES 3–5

Things I loved / learned / noticed:

_____

_____

_____

_____

Questions / things I want to research:

_____

_____

_____

_____

God Shot:

_____

_____

_____

_____

God uses the unlikely to reveal Himself at work,
to reveal His heart for the overlooked.

JUDGES 6–7

Things I loved / learned / noticed:

Questions / things I want to research:

God Shot:

JUDGES 8–9

Things I loved / learned / noticed:

Questions / things I want to research:

God Shot:

God's wrath and justice are adjacent
to His love, not in contrast to it.

JUDGES 10–12

Things I loved / learned / noticed:

Questions / things I want to research:

God Shot:

May you feel the nearness of the Lord in your brokenhearted state, and may your spirit feel somehow less crushed as you remember His great salvation.

JUDGES 13–15

Things I loved / learned / noticed:

_____

_____

_____

_____

Questions / things I want to research:

_____

_____

_____

_____

God Shot:

_____

_____

_____

_____

Praise God our sinful motives and actions
aren't big enough to ruin His plan.

JUDGES 16–18

Things I loved / learned / noticed:

_____

_____

_____

_____

Questions / things I want to research:

_____

_____

_____

_____

God Shot:

_____

_____

_____

_____

Whether we're in dire straits or in a place of
abundance, God's ready to come closer.

JUDGES 19–21

Things I loved / learned / noticed:

_____

_____

_____

_____

Questions / things I want to research:

_____

_____

_____

_____

God Shot:

_____

_____

_____

_____

When we fail to consult God and lean on our own
understanding, we almost always make a bigger mess.

RUTH 1–4

Things I loved / learned / noticed:

_____

_____

_____

_____

Questions / things I want to research:

_____

_____

_____

_____

God Shot:

_____

_____

_____

_____

Pray: O God, thank You for Your Word—for reminders of how You work
through imperfect children like me. Use me to advance Your kingdom.

1 SAMUEL 1–3

Things I loved / learned / noticed:

_____

_____

_____

_____

Questions / things I want to research:

_____

_____

_____

_____

God Shot:

_____

_____

_____

_____

"It is the Lord. Let him do what seems
to be good to him."—1 Samuel 3:18

1 SAMUEL 4–8

Things I loved / learned / noticed:

_____

_____

_____

_____

Questions / things I want to research:

_____

_____

_____

_____

God Shot:

_____

_____

_____

_____

Pray: Father, my identity is in You. Help me to be
fully at peace with being uniquely Yours.

1 SAMUEL 9–12

Things I loved / learned / noticed:

_____

_____

_____

_____

Questions / things I want to research:

_____

_____

_____

_____

God Shot:

_____

_____

_____

_____

God knows every wrong you've ever done and ever will
do, and still, He's pleased to call you His child.

1 SAMUEL 13–14

Things I loved / learned / noticed:

_____

_____

_____

_____

Questions / things I want to research:

_____

_____

_____

_____

God Shot:

_____

_____

_____

_____

Take comfort—nothing can ruin God's plan;
He's active in every tick of the clock.

1 SAMUEL 15–17

Things I loved / learned / noticed:

_____

_____

_____

_____

Questions / things I want to research:

_____

_____

_____

_____

God Shot:

_____

_____

_____

_____

"I come to you
in the name of the LORD of hosts."—1 Samuel 17:45

1 SAMUEL 18–20; PSALMS 11, 59

Things I loved / learned / noticed:

_____

_____

_____

_____

Questions / things I want to research:

_____

_____

_____

_____

God Shot:

_____

_____

_____

_____

"O my Strength, I will watch for you,
for you, O God, are my fortress."—Psalm 59:9

DAY 104

DATE

1 SAMUEL 21–24

Things I loved / learned / noticed:

_____

_____

_____

_____

Questions / things I want to research:

_____

_____

_____

_____

God Shot:

_____

_____

_____

_____

Pray: Lord, help me to accept and trust Your timing.
Guide my steps. I know You'll always be with me.

PSALMS 7, 27, 31, 34, 52

Things I loved / learned / noticed:

_____

_____

_____

_____

Questions / things I want to research:

_____

_____

_____

_____

God Shot:

_____

_____

_____

_____

"Wait for the LORD; be strong, and let your
heart take courage."—Psalm 27:14

PSALMS 56, 120, 140–142

Things I loved / learned / noticed:

_____
_____
_____
_____

Questions / things I want to research:

_____
_____
_____
_____

God Shot:

_____
_____
_____
_____

It's easy to think God is distant or unfeeling when
we endure trials, but He knows, He sees.

1 SAMUEL 25–27

Things I loved / learned / noticed:

_____

_____

_____

_____

Questions / things I want to research:

_____

_____

_____

_____

God Shot:

_____

_____

_____

_____

The wise in heart know that joy isn't found in getting
our own way—it's found in yielding to His way.

PSALMS 17, 35, 54, 63

Things I loved / learned / noticed:

_____

_____

_____

_____

Questions / things I want to research:

_____

_____

_____

_____

God Shot:

_____

_____

_____

_____

1 SAMUEL 28–31; PSALM 18

Things I loved / learned / noticed:

_____

_____

_____

_____

Questions / things I want to research:

_____

_____

_____

_____

God Shot:

_____

_____

_____

_____

Pray: Strengthen me, Lord. I don't know what the
coming days will bring, but I know I need You.

DATE

PSALMS 121, 123–125, 128–130

Things I loved / learned / noticed:

_____

_____

_____

_____

Questions / things I want to research:

_____

_____

_____

_____

God Shot:

_____

_____

_____

_____

No matter how we've walked in iniquity and rebellion,
we can come to God for forgiveness.

2 SAMUEL 1–4

Things I loved / learned / noticed:

_____

_____

_____

_____

Questions / things I want to research:

_____

_____

_____

_____

God Shot:

_____

_____

_____

_____

Pray: God, thank You that You're an approachable King
and that You love when I draw near to You.

PSALMS 6, 8–10, 14, 16, 19, 21

Things I loved / learned / noticed:

_____

_____

_____

_____

Questions / things I want to research:

_____

_____

_____

_____

God Shot:

_____

_____

_____

_____

"Let the words of my mouth and the meditation
of my heart be acceptable in your sight, O LORD,
my rock and my redeemer."—Psalm 19:14

1 CHRONICLES 1–2

Things I loved / learned / noticed:

_____

_____

_____

_____

Questions / things I want to research:

_____

_____

_____

_____

God Shot:

_____

_____

_____

_____

God uses every story, from the great
to the terrible to the person who never
does anything historically significant.

PSALMS 43–45, 49, 84–85, 87

Things I loved / learned / noticed:

_____

_____

_____

_____

Questions / things I want to research:

_____

_____

_____

_____

God Shot:

_____

_____

_____

_____

1 CHRONICLES 3–5

Things I loved / learned / noticed:

Questions / things I want to research:

God Shot:

Trust God to take all your prayers, sift them, and faithfully respond to you with what is best in each unique situation.

PSALMS 73, 77–78

Things I loved / learned / noticed:

_____

_____

_____

_____

Questions / things I want to research:

_____

_____

_____

_____

God Shot:

_____

_____

_____

_____

"I have made the Lord God my refuge,
that I may tell of all your works."—Psalm 73:28

1 CHRONICLES 6

Things I loved / learned / noticed:

Questions / things I want to research:

God Shot:

Pray: Father, You're so wise, and Your plans are perfect.
Thank You for making a plan for my restoration and
redemption—I'm so happy to be reconciled to You.

PSALMS 81, 88, 92–93

Things I loved / learned / noticed:

_____

_____

_____

_____

Questions / things I want to research:

_____

_____

_____

_____

God Shot:

_____

_____

_____

_____

God's not just the one who makes us righteous,
but He *is* our righteousness.

1 CHRONICLES 7–10

Things I loved / learned / noticed:

_____

_____

_____

_____

Questions / things I want to research:

_____

_____

_____

_____

God Shot:

_____

_____

_____

_____

Does harm happen to God's children? Absolutely. But He preserves
what is most important: our souls and our relationship with Him.

PSALMS 102–104

Things I loved / learned / noticed:

_____

_____

_____

_____

Questions / things I want to research:

_____

_____

_____

_____

God Shot:

_____

_____

_____

_____

"O Lᴏʀᴅ, how manifold are your works! In wisdom have you made them all; the earth is full of your creatures."—Psalm 104:24

2 SAMUEL 5; 1 CHRONICLES 11–12

Things I loved / learned / noticed:

_____

_____

_____

_____

Questions / things I want to research:

_____

_____

_____

_____

God Shot:

_____

_____

_____

_____

PSALM 133

Things I loved / learned / noticed:

_____

_____

_____

_____

Questions / things I want to research:

_____

_____

_____

_____

God Shot:

_____

_____

_____

_____

A peaceful life is great, but the real gift is eternal life with
God where we live under the blessings of His presence.

PSALMS 106–107

Things I loved / learned / noticed:

Questions / things I want to research:

God Shot:

"Oh give thanks to the Lord, for he is good, for his
steadfast love endures forever!"—Psalm 107:1

DATE

1 CHRONICLES 13–16

Things I loved / learned / noticed:

_____
_____
_____
_____

Questions / things I want to research:

_____
_____
_____
_____

God Shot:

_____
_____
_____
_____

Pray: Father, I give thanks for Your Spirit—our Guide and Helper.
Open my eyes and ears to Your directions. You are trustworthy.

PSALMS 1–2, 15, 22–24, 47, 68

Things I loved / learned / noticed:

_____

_____

_____

_____

Questions / things I want to research:

_____

_____

_____

_____

God Shot:

_____

_____

_____

_____

It's easy to despise stillness and waiting, but God
invites us into the calm and the quiet.

PSALMS 89, 96, 100–101, 105, 132

Things I loved / learned / noticed:

_____

_____

_____

_____

Questions / things I want to research:

_____

_____

_____

_____

God Shot:

_____

_____

_____

_____

"Serve the LORD with gladness! Come into his
presence with singing!"—Psalm 100:2

2 SAMUEL 6–7; 1 CHRONICLES 17

Things I loved / learned / noticed:

_____

_____

_____

_____

Questions / things I want to research:

_____

_____

_____

_____

God Shot:

_____

_____

_____

_____

If God says no,
it is His kindest possible answer.

PSALMS 25, 29, 33, 36, 39

Things I loved / learned / noticed:

_____

_____

_____

_____

Questions / things I want to research:

_____

_____

_____

_____

God Shot:

_____

_____

_____

_____

Pray: Lord, You have proven Yourself trustworthy. Your love is
pure, and You keep Your promises. Take over my heart.

2 SAMUEL 8–9; 1 CHRONICLES 18

Things I loved / learned / noticed:

_____

_____

_____

_____

Questions / things I want to research:

_____

_____

_____

_____

God Shot:

_____

_____

_____

_____

PSALMS 50, 53, 60, 75

Things I loved / learned / noticed:

_____

_____

_____

_____

Questions / things I want to research:

_____

_____

_____

_____

God Shot:

_____

_____

_____

_____

Gratitude is an act of remembrance. It knits our hearts to God,
which means we'll be much more likely to walk closely with Him.

2 SAMUEL 10; 1 CHRONICLES 19; PSALM 20

Things I loved / learned / noticed:

_____

_____

_____

_____

Questions / things I want to research:

_____

_____

_____

God Shot:

_____

_____

_____

God is in charge and He's trustworthy. And
because of that, we can be courageous.

PSALMS 65–67, 69–70

Things I loved / learned / noticed:

Questions / things I want to research:

God Shot:

"I am afflicted and in pain; let your salvation,
O God, set me on high!"—Psalm 69:29

2 SAMUEL 11–12; 1 CHRONICLES 20

Things I loved / learned / noticed:

_____

_____

_____

_____

Questions / things I want to research:

_____

_____

_____

_____

God Shot:

_____

_____

_____

_____

Pray: God, help me to never forget how generous
You are and how You take care of me every day.

PSALMS 32, 51, 86, 122

Things I loved / learned / noticed:

_____

_____

_____

_____

Questions / things I want to research:

_____

_____

_____

_____

God Shot:

_____

_____

_____

_____

"Create in me a clean heart, O God, and renew
a right spirit within me."—Psalm 51:10

2 SAMUEL 13–15

Things I loved / learned / noticed:

_____

_____

_____

_____

Questions / things I want to research:

_____

_____

_____

_____

God Shot:

_____

_____

_____

_____

Pray: O God, I praise Your sovereign power. When things feel out of control, remind me to seek Your direction and wisdom. I trust You.

PSALMS 3–4, 12–13, 28, 55

Things I loved / learned / noticed:

_____

_____

_____

_____

Questions / things I want to research:

_____

_____

_____

_____

God Shot:

_____

_____

_____

_____

"The Lord is my strength and my shield; in him
my heart trusts, and I am helped."—Psalm 28:7

2 SAMUEL 16–18

Things I loved / learned / noticed:

Questions / things I want to research:

God Shot:

PSALMS 26, 40, 58, 61–62, 64

Things I loved / learned / noticed:

_____

_____

_____

_____

Questions / things I want to research:

_____

_____

_____

_____

God Shot:

_____

_____

_____

_____

God delights in being the Giver—giving us ears that hear
Him and hearts that know He's where the joy is!

2 SAMUEL 19–21

Things I loved / learned / noticed:

_____

_____

_____

_____

Questions / things I want to research:

_____

_____

_____

_____

God Shot:

_____

_____

_____

_____

When we're wronged, we can trust God to work on our
behalf in the hearts of those who have wronged us.

DATE

PSALMS 5, 38, 41–42

Things I loved / learned / noticed:

_____

_____

_____

_____

Questions / things I want to research:

_____

_____

_____

_____

God Shot:

_____

_____

_____

_____

Pray: Father, restore me and raise me up. My hope is in You.

2 SAMUEL 22–23; PSALM 57

Things I loved / learned / noticed:

_____

_____

_____

_____

Questions / things I want to research:

_____

_____

_____

_____

God Shot:

_____

_____

_____

_____

PSALMS 95, 97–99

Things I loved / learned / noticed:

_____

_____

_____

_____

Questions / things I want to research:

_____

_____

_____

_____

God Shot:

_____

_____

_____

_____

2 SAMUEL 24; 1 CHRONICLES 21–22; PSALM 30

Things I loved / learned / noticed:

_____
_____
_____
_____
_____

Questions / things I want to research:

_____
_____
_____
_____

God Shot:

_____
_____
_____
_____

Sin never gets to win against God and His people—
it ultimately serves God's purposes somehow.

PSALMS 108–110

Things I loved / learned / noticed:

Questions / things I want to research:

God Shot:

1 CHRONICLES 23–25

Things I loved / learned / noticed:

Questions / things I want to research:

God Shot:

PSALMS 131, 138–139, 143–145

Things I loved / learned / noticed:

_____

_____

_____

_____

Questions / things I want to research:

_____

_____

_____

_____

God Shot:

_____

_____

_____

_____

"Search me, O God, and know my heart! Try me
and know my thoughts!"—Psalm 139:23

1 CHRONICLES 26–29; PSALM 127

Things I loved / learned / noticed:

Questions / things I want to research:

God Shot:

God is the source of all good things.

PSALMS 111–118

Things I loved / learned / noticed:

_____

_____

_____

_____

Questions / things I want to research:

_____

_____

_____

_____

God Shot:

_____

_____

_____

_____

"The Lord is on my side;
I will not fear."—Psalm 118:6

1 KINGS 1–2; PSALMS 37, 71, 94

Things I loved / learned / noticed:

_____

_____

_____

_____

Questions / things I want to research:

_____

_____

_____

_____

God Shot:

_____

_____

_____

_____

What a gift to know that all our sins—past, present, future, intentional,
confessed, and accidental—are covered by the blood of Christ.

DAY 150

PSALM 119

Things I loved / learned / noticed:

_____

_____

_____

_____

Questions / things I want to research:

_____

_____

_____

_____

God Shot:

_____

_____

_____

_____

Pray: Father, direct my heart. Teach me Your ways and
give me understanding so that I will live wisely.

1 KINGS 3–4

Things I loved / learned / noticed:

Questions / things I want to research:

God Shot:

2 CHRONICLES 1; PSALM 72

Things I loved / learned / noticed:

Questions / things I want to research:

God Shot:

"Blessed be the Lord, the God of Israel, who alone
does wondrous things."—Psalm 72:18

SONG OF SOLOMON 1–8

Things I loved / learned / noticed:

_____

_____

_____

_____

Questions / things I want to research:

_____

_____

_____

_____

God Shot:

_____

_____

_____

_____

Our Creator had good things in mind when He
invented relationships, marriage, and sex.

PROVERBS 1–3

Things I loved / learned / noticed:

_____

_____

_____

_____

Questions / things I want to research:

_____

_____

_____

_____

God Shot:

_____

_____

_____

_____

"The fear of the Lord is the beginning of knowledge; fools despise wisdom and instruction."—Proverbs 1:7

PROVERBS 4–6

Things I loved / learned / noticed:

_____

_____

_____

_____

Questions / things I want to research:

_____

_____

_____

_____

God Shot:

_____

_____

_____

_____

May God's Spirit empower us
to be more like Him.

PROVERBS 7–9

Things I loved / learned / noticed:

_____

_____

_____

_____

Questions / things I want to research:

_____

_____

_____

_____

God Shot:

_____

_____

_____

_____

Wisdom is the path to life.
God delights in wisdom.

PROVERBS 10–12

Things I loved / learned / noticed:

Questions / things I want to research:

God Shot:

Christ's death covers not only our rebellious moments,
but also the selfish motives behind our so-called good actions.

PROVERBS 13–15

Things I loved / learned / noticed:

_____

_____

_____

_____

Questions / things I want to research:

_____

_____

_____

_____

God Shot:

_____

_____

_____

_____

Pray: Lord, draw me near.
If I've done something to push You away, correct me.
I treasure Your peace and power.

PROVERBS 16–18

Things I loved / learned / noticed:

Questions / things I want to research:

God Shot:

When discouragement threatens to take hold, or fear taunts
you, or regret knocks on your door, take comfort in God's sweet
sovereignty—that He's working out His plan for good.

PROVERBS 19–21

Things I loved / learned / noticed:

Questions / things I want to research:

God Shot:

PROVERBS 22–24

Things I loved / learned / noticed:

_____

_____

_____

_____

Questions / things I want to research:

_____

_____

_____

_____

God Shot:

_____

_____

_____

_____

Steer clear of things that ensnare you.
What things take your eyes and affections off God?

1 KINGS 5–6; 2 CHRONICLES 2–3

Things I loved / learned / noticed:

_____

_____

_____

_____

Questions / things I want to research:

_____

_____

_____

God Shot:

_____

_____

_____

_____

Pray: Thank You, Lord, that Your presence doesn't
require a temple. You meet me where I am.

1 KINGS 7; 2 CHRONICLES 4

Things I loved / learned / noticed:

_____

_____

_____

_____

Questions / things I want to research:

_____

_____

_____

_____

God Shot:

_____

_____

_____

_____

God doesn't dwell in buildings.
He dwells in His people.

1 KINGS 8; 2 CHRONICLES 5

Things I loved / learned / noticed:

Questions / things I want to research:

God Shot:

"O Lord, God of Israel, there is no God like you, in heaven above or on earth beneath, keeping covenant and showing steadfast love to your servants who walk before you with all their heart."—1 Kings 8:23

2 CHRONICLES 6–7; PSALM 136

Things I loved / learned / noticed:

Questions / things I want to research:

God Shot:

How remarkable it is that God comes down to live with us,
to concentrate His perfect presence in the midst of our wickedness.

DATE

PSALMS 134, 146–150

Things I loved / learned / noticed:

_____

_____

_____

_____

Questions / things I want to research:

_____

_____

_____

_____

God Shot:

_____

_____

_____

_____

Because of God's sovereignty over all things, we can
trust Him—we can open our hand and loosen our grip.

1 KINGS 9; 2 CHRONICLES 8

Things I loved / learned / noticed:

_____

_____

_____

_____

Questions / things I want to research:

_____

_____

_____

_____

God Shot:

_____

_____

_____

_____

Wickedness deserves punishment.
Yet God still has mercy.

DATE

PROVERBS 25–26

Things I loved / learned / noticed:

_____

_____

_____

_____

Questions / things I want to research:

_____

_____

_____

_____

God Shot:

_____

_____

_____

_____

Any time God conceals things from us, we can rest
assured that it's ultimately in our best interest.

PROVERBS 27–29

Things I loved / learned / noticed:

Questions / things I want to research:

God Shot:

ECCLESIASTES 1–6

Things I loved / learned / noticed:

_____

_____

_____

_____

Questions / things I want to research:

_____

_____

_____

_____

God Shot:

_____

_____

_____

_____

Everything God sets in motion
is immovable—it lasts.

ECCLESIASTES 7–12

Things I loved / learned / noticed:

Questions / things I want to research:

God Shot:

We can't understand God's ways, but they govern everything
we do, so it's best and wisest to yield to Him.

1 KINGS 10–11; 2 CHRONICLES 9

Things I loved / learned / noticed:

Questions / things I want to research:

God Shot:

PROVERBS 30–31

Things I loved / learned / noticed:

_____

_____

_____

_____

Questions / things I want to research:

_____

_____

_____

_____

God Shot:

_____

_____

_____

_____

To live in the fear of the LORD means
we don't live in fear of tomorrow.

1 KINGS 12–14

Things I loved / learned / noticed:

_____

_____

_____

_____

Questions / things I want to research:

_____

_____

_____

_____

God Shot:

_____

_____

_____

_____

Obey the voice of God,
not the voice of man.

2 CHRONICLES 10–12

Things I loved / learned / noticed:

_____

_____

_____

_____

Questions / things I want to research:

_____

_____

_____

_____

God Shot:

_____

_____

_____

_____

God's plan isn't always easy, but we gain things in
surrendering to Him that we'd never have otherwise.

1 KINGS 15; 2 CHRONICLES 13–16

Things I loved / learned / noticed:

_____

_____

_____

_____

Questions / things I want to research:

_____

_____

_____

_____

God Shot:

_____

_____

_____

_____

"If you seek him, he will be found by you."
—2 Chronicles 15:2

1 KINGS 16; 2 CHRONICLES 17

Things I loved / learned / noticed:

_____

_____

_____

_____

Questions / things I want to research:

_____

_____

_____

_____

God Shot:

_____

_____

_____

_____

Our God is bigger than we realize, accomplishing far more than
meets the eye, because He does a lot of His work at a heart level.

1 KINGS 17–19

Things I loved / learned / noticed:

_____

_____

_____

_____

Questions / things I want to research:

_____

_____

_____

_____

God Shot:

_____

_____

_____

_____

Pray: God, I'm in awe of You—You're all powerful, but You're also personal and intimate. Thank You that You understand and care about my emotions.

1 KINGS 20–21

Things I loved / learned / noticed:

Questions / things I want to research:

God Shot:

God loves to show mercy to people, even the most
wicked among us. He's eager to forgive.

DATE

1 KINGS 22; 2 CHRONICLES 18

Things I loved / learned / noticed:

_____

_____

_____

_____

Questions / things I want to research:

_____

_____

_____

_____

God Shot:

_____

_____

_____

_____

Nothing is random where God is concerned. He's so intentional.

2 CHRONICLES 19–23

Things I loved / learned / noticed:

_____

_____

_____

_____

Questions / things I want to research:

_____

_____

_____

_____

God Shot:

_____

_____

_____

_____

OBADIAH 1; PSALMS 82–83

Things I loved / learned / noticed:

_____

_____

_____

_____

Questions / things I want to research:

_____

_____

_____

_____

God Shot:

_____

_____

_____

_____

"Arise, O God, judge the earth;
for you shall inherit all the nations!"—Psalm 82:8

2 KINGS 1–4

Things I loved / learned / noticed:

_____

_____

_____

_____

Questions / things I want to research:

_____

_____

_____

_____

God Shot:

_____

_____

_____

_____

Regardless of whether your next battle ends in a
victory or a setback, He's where the joy is!

2 KINGS 5–8

Things I loved / learned / noticed:

Questions / things I want to research:

God Shot:

We may doubt and resist, but God persists,
and God always gets what He wants.

2 KINGS 9–11

Things I loved / learned / noticed:

_____

_____

_____

_____

Questions / things I want to research:

_____

_____

_____

_____

God Shot:

_____

_____

_____

_____

Pray: Father, help me to obey You fully, not just
in part, and keep my gaze fixed on You.

2 KINGS 12–13; 2 CHRONICLES 24

Things I loved / learned / noticed:

Questions / things I want to research:

God Shot:

God's goodness isn't contingent on our strengths
or even on the strength of our faith.

2 KINGS 14; 2 CHRONICLES 25

Things I loved / learned / noticed:

_____

_____

_____

_____

Questions / things I want to research:

_____

_____

_____

_____

God Shot:

_____

_____

_____

_____

Both victory and loss are in God's hands.
May we aim to be on His side, for He is always victorious.

JONAH 1–4

Things I loved / learned / noticed:

_____

_____

_____

_____

Questions / things I want to research:

_____

_____

_____

_____

God Shot:

_____

_____

_____

_____

"When God saw what they did, how they turned from their
evil way, God relented of the disaster that he had said he
would do to them, and he did not do it."—Jonah 3:10

2 KINGS 15; 2 CHRONICLES 26

Things I loved / learned / noticed:

Questions / things I want to research:

God Shot:

Pray: Father, when You give me success,
help me not to become prideful,
but to remember that all I have comes from You.

ISAIAH 1–4

Things I loved / learned / noticed:

_____

_____

_____

_____

Questions / things I want to research:

_____

_____

_____

_____

God Shot:

_____

_____

_____

_____

Despite our fearful bargaining, idolatry, selfishness,
and vanity, God still wants to unite Himself with us.

ISAIAH 5–8

Things I loved / learned / noticed:

_____

_____

_____

_____

Questions / things I want to research:

_____

_____

_____

_____

God Shot:

_____

_____

_____

_____

"Woe to those who call evil good and good evil."
—Isaiah 5:20

AMOS 1–5

Things I loved / learned / noticed:

_____

_____

_____

_____

Questions / things I want to research:

_____

_____

_____

_____

God Shot:

_____

_____

_____

_____

God's judgment for sin is always deserved
and often even delayed, because He's patient.

AMOS 6–9

Things I loved / learned / noticed:

_____

_____

_____

_____

Questions / things I want to research:

_____

_____

_____

_____

God Shot:

_____

_____

_____

_____

God's goal in punishment is always restoration. His discipline
is part of His love, just like with any good parent.

2 CHRONICLES 27; ISAIAH 9–12

Things I loved / learned / noticed:

Questions / things I want to research:

God Shot:

MICAH 1–7

Things I loved / learned / noticed:

_____

_____

_____

_____

Questions / things I want to research:

_____

_____

_____

_____

God Shot:

_____

_____

_____

_____

When God increases and we decrease,
that's where we find our greatest peace.

2 CHRONICLES 28; 2 KINGS 16–17

Things I loved / learned / noticed:

_____

_____

_____

_____

Questions / things I want to research:

_____

_____

_____

_____

God Shot:

_____

_____

_____

_____

Pray: God, thank You for Your patience with me. Help me to hear
and obey when You warn me about a pattern of sin in my life.

ISAIAH 13–17

Things I loved / learned / noticed:

_____

_____

_____

_____

Questions / things I want to research:

_____

_____

_____

_____

God Shot:

_____

_____

_____

_____

Seeing God mourn over having to punish sin shows us
that He's a real person with a real personality.

ISAIAH 18–22

Things I loved / learned / noticed:

_____

_____

_____

_____

Questions / things I want to research:

_____

_____

_____

_____

God Shot:

_____

_____

_____

_____

God causes His Word
to bear fruit in our lives!

ISAIAH 23–27

Things I loved / learned / noticed:

_____

_____

_____

_____

Questions / things I want to research:

_____

_____

_____

_____

God Shot:

_____

_____

_____

_____

"O Lord, you will ordain peace for us, for you have
indeed done for us all our works."—Isaiah 26:12

2 KINGS 18; 2 CHRONICLES 29–31; PSALM 48

Things I loved / learned / noticed:

Questions / things I want to research:

God Shot:

"The Lord your God is gracious and merciful and will not turn away his face from you, if you return to him."—2 Chronicles 30:9

HOSEA 1–7

Things I loved / learned / noticed:

Questions / things I want to research:

God Shot:

DATE

HOSEA 8–14

Things I loved / learned / noticed:

_____

_____

_____

_____

Questions / things I want to research:

_____

_____

_____

_____

God Shot:

_____

_____

_____

_____

God's heart is to heal and save His children,
meeting us in our sin with open arms.

ISAIAH 28–30

Things I loved / learned / noticed:

_____

_____

_____

_____

Questions / things I want to research:

_____

_____

_____

_____

God Shot:

_____

_____

_____

_____

"Therefore the Lord waits to be gracious to you."
—Isaiah 30:18

DATE

ISAIAH 31–34

Things I loved / learned / noticed:

_____

_____

_____

_____

Questions / things I want to research:

_____

_____

_____

_____

God Shot:

_____

_____

_____

_____

The active presence of God's Spirit brings justice and righteousness.

ISAIAH 35–36

Things I loved / learned / noticed:

Questions / things I want to research:

God Shot:

DATE

ISAIAH 37–39; PSALM 76

Things I loved / learned / noticed:

_____

_____

_____

_____

Questions / things I want to research:

_____

_____

_____

_____

God Shot:

_____

_____

_____

_____

God has set His very good plan in motion,
and He's using it to bless us and glorify Himself.

ISAIAH 40–43

Things I loved / learned / noticed:

_____

_____

_____

_____

Questions / things I want to research:

_____

_____

_____

_____

God Shot:

_____

_____

_____

_____

"They who wait for the LORD shall renew their strength;
they shall mount up with wings like eagles; they shall run and
not be weary; they shall walk and not faint."—Isaiah 40:31

ISAIAH 44–48

Things I loved / learned / noticed:

_____

_____

_____

_____

Questions / things I want to research:

_____

_____

_____

_____

God Shot:

_____

_____

_____

_____

God's consistency is so comforting
when we stop to recall it.

2 KINGS 19; PSALMS 46, 80, 135

Things I loved / learned / noticed:

_____

_____

_____

_____

Questions / things I want to research:

_____

_____

_____

_____

God Shot:

_____

_____

_____

_____

"God is our refuge and strength,
a very present help in trouble."—Psalm 46:1

ISAIAH 49–53

Things I loved / learned / noticed:

_____

_____

_____

_____

Questions / things I want to research:

_____

_____

_____

_____

God Shot:

_____

_____

_____

_____

Pray: Jesus, Messiah, I'm in awe of how You willingly suffered to serve and save us. Thank You that I can be at peace because You have redeemed me.

ISAIAH 54–58

Things I loved / learned / noticed:

_____

_____

_____

_____

Questions / things I want to research:

_____

_____

_____

_____

God Shot:

_____

_____

_____

_____

It's always been and still is about the relationship,
about the love, between God and His people.

DATE

ISAIAH 59–63

Things I loved / learned / noticed:

_____

_____

_____

_____

Questions / things I want to research:

_____

_____

_____

_____

God Shot:

_____

_____

_____

_____

To some, it's challenging to hear that God might want to
bless people we hate or people who have hurt us.

ISAIAH 64–66

Things I loved / learned / noticed:

Questions / things I want to research:

God Shot:

"We are the clay, and you are our potter; we are all the work of your hand. Be not so terribly angry, O LORD, and remember not iniquity forever."—Isaiah 64:8–9

DATE

2 KINGS 20–21

Things I loved / learned / noticed:

_____

_____

_____

_____

Questions / things I want to research:

_____

_____

_____

_____

God Shot:

_____

_____

_____

_____

Often our prayers are pleas to avoid pain,
but pain is often where we draw near to God.

2 CHRONICLES 32–33

Things I loved / learned / noticed:

Questions / things I want to research:

God Shot:

NAHUM 1–3

Things I loved / learned / noticed:

_____

_____

_____

_____

Questions / things I want to research:

_____

_____

_____

_____

God Shot:

_____

_____

_____

_____

God isn't blind to injustice or oppression.

2 KINGS 22–23; 2 CHRONICLES 34–35

Things I loved / learned / noticed:

_____

_____

_____

_____

Questions / things I want to research:

_____

_____

_____

_____

God Shot:

_____

_____

_____

_____

God can use anyone and everyone to point to Himself and His truth.

ZEPHANIAH 1–3

Things I loved / learned / noticed:

_____

_____

_____

_____

Questions / things I want to research:

_____

_____

_____

_____

God Shot:

_____

_____

_____

_____

God loves to banish the fears of His people.

JEREMIAH 1–3

Things I loved / learned / noticed:

_____

_____

_____

_____

Questions / things I want to research:

_____

_____

_____

_____

God Shot:

_____

_____

_____

_____

Pray: God, thank You that my life is important to You.
Before I was born, You had a plan and a purpose for me.

DATE

JEREMIAH 4–6

Things I loved / learned / noticed:

_____

_____

_____

_____

Questions / things I want to research:

_____

_____

_____

_____

God Shot:

_____

_____

_____

_____

Sin is a thief—
it steals good things from you.

JEREMIAH 7–9

Things I loved / learned / noticed:

_____

_____

_____

_____

Questions / things I want to research:

_____

_____

_____

_____

God Shot:

_____

_____

_____

_____

"I am the LORD who practices steadfast love, justice,
and righteousness in the earth."—Jeremiah 9:24

JEREMIAH 10–13

Things I loved / learned / noticed:

_____

_____

_____

_____

Questions / things I want to research:

_____

_____

_____

_____

God Shot:

_____

_____

_____

_____

God is with us in every moment—not just in
destinations and arrivals, but in steps.

JEREMIAH 14–17

Things I loved / learned / noticed:

_____

_____

_____

_____

Questions / things I want to research:

_____

_____

_____

_____

God Shot:

_____

_____

_____

_____

What a gift it is that God wants
to spend time with us.

DATE

JEREMIAH 18–22

Things I loved / learned / noticed:

Questions / things I want to research:

God Shot:

JEREMIAH 23–25

Things I loved / learned / noticed:

_____

_____

_____

_____

Questions / things I want to research:

_____

_____

_____

_____

God Shot:

_____

_____

_____

_____

We have no righteousness of our own,
but our God-King-Savior came down to give us His.

JEREMIAH 26–29

Things I loved / learned / noticed:

_____

_____

_____

_____

Questions / things I want to research:

_____

_____

_____

_____

God Shot:

_____

_____

_____

_____

JEREMIAH 30–31

Things I loved / learned / noticed:

_____

_____

_____

_____

Questions / things I want to research:

_____

_____

_____

_____

God Shot:

_____

_____

_____

_____

May we always be satisfied because we have God.

JEREMIAH 32–34

Things I loved / learned / noticed:

_____

_____

_____

_____

Questions / things I want to research:

_____

_____

_____

_____

God Shot:

_____

_____

_____

_____

"Call to me and I will answer you, and will tell you great and hidden things that you have not known."—Jeremiah 33:3

JEREMIAH 35–37

Things I loved / learned / noticed:

_____

_____

_____

_____

Questions / things I want to research:

_____

_____

_____

_____

God Shot:

_____

_____

_____

_____

Pray: Father, may my decisions, my relationships, my time be
investments in the eternal. I want to build with You something that lasts.

JEREMIAH 38–40; PSALMS 74, 79

Things I loved / learned / noticed:

_____

_____

_____

_____

Questions / things I want to research:

_____

_____

_____

_____

God Shot:

_____

_____

_____

_____

"Arise, O God, defend your cause."—Psalm 74:22

2 KINGS 24–25; 2 CHRONICLES 36

Things I loved / learned / noticed:

_____

_____

_____

_____

Questions / things I want to research:

_____

_____

_____

_____

God Shot:

_____

_____

_____

_____

God clothes us in robes of righteousness and seats us at His table.

HABAKKUK 1–3

Things I loved / learned / noticed:

Questions / things I want to research:

God Shot:

Resolve to wait for God's timing.
Trust Him and His process.

JEREMIAH 41–45

Things I loved / learned / noticed:

_____

_____

_____

_____

Questions / things I want to research:

_____

_____

_____

_____

God Shot:

_____

_____

_____

_____

JEREMIAH 46–48

Things I loved / learned / noticed:

Questions / things I want to research:

God Shot:

Awareness of God's nearness
is the antidote to fear.

JEREMIAH 49–50

Things I loved / learned / noticed:

_____

_____

_____

_____

Questions / things I want to research:

_____

_____

_____

_____

God Shot:

_____

_____

_____

_____

Pray: Thank You, Lord, for dying on the cross and paying
the penalty for my sins. Though I have no righteousness
of my own, I'm made righteous by You.

JEREMIAH 51–52

Things I loved / learned / noticed:

_____

_____

_____

_____

Questions / things I want to research:

_____

_____

_____

_____

God Shot:

_____

_____

_____

_____

LAMENTATIONS 1–2

Things I loved / learned / noticed:

_____

_____

_____

_____

Questions / things I want to research:

_____

_____

_____

_____

God Shot:

_____

_____

_____

_____

Our God engages with the good, the bad, and the ugly in our hearts.

LAMENTATIONS 3–5

Things I loved / learned / noticed:

_____

_____

_____

_____

Questions / things I want to research:

_____

_____

_____

_____

God Shot:

_____

_____

_____

_____

"The LORD is good to those who wait for him,
to the soul who seeks him."—Lamentations 3:25

EZEKIEL 1–4

Things I loved / learned / noticed:

_____

_____

_____

_____

Questions / things I want to research:

_____

_____

_____

_____

God Shot:

_____

_____

_____

_____

Pray: God, You're so purposeful in how You make each human being.
I praise You for Your perfect design and kind heart.

EZEKIEL 5–8

Things I loved / learned / noticed:

_____

_____

_____

_____

Questions / things I want to research:

_____

_____

_____

_____

God Shot:

_____

_____

_____

_____

In the end, everyone will know who God is, but not everyone will submit to Him and love Him. Those who do are the ones adopted into His family.

EZEKIEL 9–12

Things I loved / learned / noticed:

_____

_____

_____

_____

Questions / things I want to research:

_____

_____

_____

_____

God Shot:

_____

_____

_____

_____

God followed His people in the land of their exile,
pursuing them still. Even in exile, He's our sanctuary.

EZEKIEL 13–15

Things I loved / learned / noticed:

_____

_____

_____

_____

Questions / things I want to research:

_____

_____

_____

_____

God Shot:

_____

_____

_____

_____

God doesn't just care about our eternal destination,
He cares about the peace we carry with us day by day.

EZEKIEL 16–17

Things I loved / learned / noticed:

Questions / things I want to research:

God Shot:

"I am the LORD; I have spoken, and I will do it."
—Ezekiel 17:24

EZEKIEL 18–20

Things I loved / learned / noticed:

_____

_____

_____

_____

Questions / things I want to research:

_____

_____

_____

_____

_____

God Shot:

_____

_____

_____

_____

Pray: Father, may my faith be vibrant, and may the good works that
are evidence of my faith flow naturally from my love for You.

EZEKIEL 21–22

Things I loved / learned / noticed:

_____

_____

_____

_____

Questions / things I want to research:

_____

_____

_____

_____

God Shot:

_____

_____

_____

_____

Sin can affect the intimacy of our relationship with God, but
it doesn't affect the *status* of our relationship with God.

EZEKIEL 23–24

Things I loved / learned / noticed:

_____

_____

_____

_____

Questions / things I want to research:

_____

_____

_____

_____

God Shot:

_____

_____

_____

_____

EZEKIEL 25–27

Things I loved / learned / noticed:

_____

_____

_____

_____

Questions / things I want to research:

_____

_____

_____

_____

God Shot:

_____

_____

_____

_____

EZEKIEL 28–30

Things I loved / learned / noticed:

Questions / things I want to research:

God Shot:

EZEKIEL 31–33

Things I loved / learned / noticed:

_____

_____

_____

_____

Questions / things I want to research:

_____

_____

_____

_____

God Shot:

_____

_____

_____

_____

God's delight, His joy,
is expressed in saving the wicked.

EZEKIEL 34–36

Things I loved / learned / noticed:

_____

_____

_____

_____

Questions / things I want to research:

_____

_____

_____

_____

God Shot:

_____

_____

_____

_____

EZEKIEL 37–39

Things I loved / learned / noticed:

Questions / things I want to research:

God Shot:

EZEKIEL 40–42

Things I loved / learned / noticed:

Questions / things I want to research:

God Shot:

EZEKIEL 43–45

Things I loved / learned / noticed:

_____

_____

_____

_____

Questions / things I want to research:

_____

_____

_____

_____

God Shot:

_____

_____

_____

Draw near to God, knowing every step closer
will fuel your love and delight in Him.

EZEKIEL 46–48

Things I loved / learned / noticed:

_____

_____

_____

_____

Questions / things I want to research:

_____

_____

_____

_____

God Shot:

_____

_____

_____

_____

Pray: God, thank You that as I spend time with You,
You work in me to make me more like You.

JOEL 1–3

Things I loved / learned / noticed:

_____

_____

_____

_____

Questions / things I want to research:

_____

_____

_____

_____

God Shot:

_____

_____

_____

_____

The more we know God and His Word,
the more hopeful we'll be.

DANIEL 1–3

Things I loved / learned / noticed:

_____

_____

_____

_____

Questions / things I want to research:

_____

_____

_____

_____

God Shot:

_____

_____

_____

_____

"Blessed be the name of God forever and ever,
to whom belong wisdom and might."—Daniel 2:20

DANIEL 4–6

Things I loved / learned / noticed:

_____

_____

_____

_____

Questions / things I want to research:

_____

_____

_____

_____

God Shot:

_____

_____

_____

_____

"He is the living God, enduring forever;
his kingdom shall never be destroyed."—Daniel 6:26

DANIEL 7–9

Things I loved / learned / noticed:

_____

_____

_____

_____

Questions / things I want to research:

_____

_____

_____

_____

God Shot:

_____

_____

_____

_____

Pray: God, thank You for Your Word. Your plans have always
been and will always be perfect. You can be trusted.

DANIEL 10-12

Things I loved / learned / noticed:

Questions / things I want to research:

God Shot:

EZRA 1–3

Things I loved / learned / noticed:

_____

_____

_____

_____

Questions / things I want to research:

_____

_____

_____

_____

God Shot:

_____

_____

_____

_____

God works even in the hearts of His enemies to bless His people.

EZRA 4–6; PSALM 137

Things I loved / learned / noticed:

_____

_____

_____

_____

Questions / things I want to research:

_____

_____

_____

_____

God Shot:

_____

_____

_____

_____

God can handle our anger and grief.

HAGGAI 1–2

Things I loved / learned / noticed:

_____

_____

_____

_____

Questions / things I want to research:

_____

_____

_____

_____

God Shot:

_____

_____

_____

_____

No matter what is destroyed, God can rebuild.

ZECHARIAH 1–4

Things I loved / learned / noticed:

_____

_____

_____

_____

Questions / things I want to research:

_____

_____

_____

_____

God Shot:

_____

_____

_____

_____

DATE

ZECHARIAH 5–9

Things I loved / learned / noticed:

_____

_____

_____

_____

Questions / things I want to research:

_____

_____

_____

_____

God Shot:

_____

_____

_____

_____

ZECHARIAH 10–14

Things I loved / learned / noticed:

_____

_____

_____

_____

Questions / things I want to research:

_____

_____

_____

_____

God Shot:

_____

_____

_____

_____

Jesus is the shepherd
and the sacrifice.

DATE

ESTHER 1–5

Things I loved / learned / noticed:

_____

_____

_____

_____

Questions / things I want to research:

_____

_____

_____

_____

God Shot:

_____

_____

_____

_____

Pray: God, thank You that even in terrible circumstances You are
at work in the background. You're my only and best hope.

ESTHER 6–10

Things I loved / learned / noticed:

Questions / things I want to research:

God Shot:

God is always at work, fulfilling His promises for
your good and His glory. He can be trusted.

EZRA 7–10

Things I loved / learned / noticed:

_____

_____

_____

_____

Questions / things I want to research:

_____

_____

_____

_____

God Shot:

_____

_____

_____

_____

"I took courage, for the hand of the LORD
my God was on me."—Ezra 7:28

NEHEMIAH 1–5

Things I loved / learned / noticed:

_____

_____

_____

_____

Questions / things I want to research:

_____

_____

_____

_____

God Shot:

_____

_____

_____

_____

What God initiates,
He will sustain and He will fulfill.

NEHEMIAH 6–7

Things I loved / learned / noticed:

_____

_____

_____

_____

Questions / things I want to research:

_____

_____

_____

_____

God Shot:

_____

_____

_____

_____

NEHEMIAH 8–10

Things I loved / learned / noticed:

_____

_____

_____

_____

Questions / things I want to research:

_____

_____

_____

_____

God Shot:

_____

_____

_____

_____

Pray: Lord, You're so patient and persistent. When I sin, when I ignore You, You don't give up on me. Thank You.

NEHEMIAH 11–13; PSALM 126

Things I loved / learned / noticed:

Questions / things I want to research:

God Shot:

God works at a heart level. He produces a joy
in us that we wouldn't have otherwise.

MALACHI 1–4

Things I loved / learned / noticed:

_____

_____

_____

_____

Questions / things I want to research:

_____

_____

_____

_____

God Shot:

_____

_____

_____

_____

"For I the LORD do not change."
—Malachi 3:6

LUKE 1; JOHN 1

Things I loved / learned / noticed:

_____

_____

_____

_____

Questions / things I want to research:

_____

_____

_____

_____

God Shot:

_____

_____

_____

_____

"And the Word became flesh and dwelt among us."—John 1:14

MATTHEW 1; LUKE 2

Things I loved / learned / noticed:

_____

_____

_____

_____

Questions / things I want to research:

_____

_____

_____

_____

God Shot:

_____

_____

_____

_____

God draws near to His people through His Word and through His Spirit.

MATTHEW 2

Things I loved / learned / noticed:

_____

_____

_____

_____

Questions / things I want to research:

_____

_____

_____

_____

God Shot:

_____

_____

_____

_____

Pray: O Lord, my Protector. I know struggles will
come my way, but I trust You. I'm never alone.

MATTHEW 3; MARK 1; LUKE 3

Things I loved / learned / noticed:

Questions / things I want to research:

God Shot:

MATTHEW 4; LUKE 4–5

Things I loved / learned / noticed:

_____

_____

_____

_____

Questions / things I want to research:

_____

_____

_____

_____

God Shot:

_____

_____

_____

_____

Jesus seeks the unwanted and the unloved.

JOHN 2–4

Things I loved / learned / noticed:

_____

_____

_____

_____

Questions / things I want to research:

_____

_____

_____

_____

God Shot:

_____

_____

_____

_____

Jesus is the life giver and the law fulfiller.

MATTHEW 8; MARK 2

Things I loved / learned / noticed:

_____

_____

_____

_____

Questions / things I want to research:

_____

_____

_____

_____

God Shot:

_____

_____

_____

_____

"[Jesus] said to them, 'Those who are well have no
need of a physician, but those who are sick. I came not
to call the righteous, but sinners.'"—Mark 2:17

JOHN 5

Things I loved / learned / noticed:

_____

_____

_____

_____

Questions / things I want to research:

_____

_____

_____

_____

God Shot:

_____

_____

_____

_____

"Jesus answered them,
'My Father is working until now, and I am working.'"
—John 5:17

MATTHEW 12; MARK 3; LUKE 6

Things I loved / learned / noticed:

Questions / things I want to research:

God Shot:

MATTHEW 5–7

Things I loved / learned / noticed:

_____

_____

_____

_____

Questions / things I want to research:

_____

_____

_____

_____

God Shot:

_____

_____

_____

_____

Life in the kingdom begins with recognizing
your desperate need for God.

DATE

MATTHEW 9; LUKE 7

Things I loved / learned / noticed:

_____

_____

_____

_____

Questions / things I want to research:

_____

_____

_____

_____

God Shot:

_____

_____

_____

_____

The more we see our spiritual poverty, the more we'll
be able to grasp all the blessings of knowing God.

MATTHEW 11

Things I loved / learned / noticed:

Questions / things I want to research:

God Shot:

LUKE 11

Things I loved / learned / noticed:

_____

_____

_____

_____

Questions / things I want to research:

_____

_____

_____

_____

God Shot:

_____

_____

_____

_____

"Ask, and it will be given to you; seek, and you will find;
knock, and it will be opened to you."—Luke 11:9

MATTHEW 13; LUKE 8

Things I loved / learned / noticed:

_____

_____

_____

_____

Questions / things I want to research:

_____

_____

_____

_____

God Shot:

_____

_____

_____

_____

Trials reveal our hearts—are we only after God's
blessings, or are we truly after God Himself?

MARK 4–5

Things I loved / learned / noticed:

_____

_____

_____

_____

Questions / things I want to research:

_____

_____

_____

_____

God Shot:

_____

_____

_____

_____

MATTHEW 10

Things I loved / learned / noticed:

_____

_____

_____

_____

Questions / things I want to research:

_____

_____

_____

_____

God Shot:

_____

_____

_____

_____

Pray: Thank You, Lord, for Your all-encompassing care. I know I
can come to You with every concern, and You'll always answer.

MATTHEW 14; MARK 6; LUKE 9

Things I loved / learned / noticed:

_____

_____

_____

_____

Questions / things I want to research:

_____

_____

_____

_____

God Shot:

_____

_____

_____

_____

"He sat down and called the twelve. And he said to them, 'If anyone would be first, he must be last of all and servant of all.'"—Mark 9:35

JOHN 6

Things I loved / learned / noticed:

_____

_____

_____

_____

Questions / things I want to research:

_____

_____

_____

_____

God Shot:

_____

_____

_____

_____

MATTHEW 15; MARK 7

Things I loved / learned / noticed:

Questions / things I want to research:

God Shot:

MATTHEW 16; MARK 8

Things I loved / learned / noticed:

Questions / things I want to research:

God Shot:

Nothing you encounter today
can stop God's kingdom.

MATTHEW 17; MARK 9

Things I loved / learned / noticed:

_____

_____

_____

_____

Questions / things I want to research:

_____

_____

_____

_____

God Shot:

_____

_____

_____

_____

God wants us to ask Him for help
and to rely on Him.

MATTHEW 18

Things I loved / learned / noticed:

_____

_____

_____

_____

Questions / things I want to research:

_____

_____

_____

_____

God Shot:

_____

_____

_____

_____

"Whoever humbles himself like this child
is the greatest in the kingdom of heaven."—Matthew 18:4

DATE

JOHN 7–8

Things I loved / learned / noticed:

_____

_____

_____

_____

Questions / things I want to research:

_____

_____

_____

_____

God Shot:

_____

_____

_____

_____

Jesus is the Light of the World.

JOHN 9–10

Things I loved / learned / noticed:

_____

_____

_____

_____

Questions / things I want to research:

_____

_____

_____

_____

God Shot:

_____

_____

_____

_____

"I give them eternal life, and they will never perish, and no one will snatch them out of my hand."—John 10:28

LUKE 10

Things I loved / learned / noticed:

_____

_____

_____

_____

Questions / things I want to research:

_____

_____

_____

_____

God Shot:

_____

_____

_____

_____

Pray: God, make me a conduit of Your love to everyone I encounter today—especially the people who are the hardest to love. Thank You that it's Your Spirit working through me to accomplish this.

LUKE 12–13

Things I loved / learned / noticed:

Questions / things I want to research:

God Shot:

Fruit takes time, so God tends to us,
waters us, and fertilizes us.

LUKE 14–15

Things I loved / learned / noticed:

_____

_____

_____

_____

Questions / things I want to research:

_____

_____

_____

_____

God Shot:

_____

_____

_____

_____

"I tell you, there will be more joy in heaven over one sinner who repents than over ninety-nine righteous persons who need no repentance."—Luke 15:7

LUKE 16–17

Things I loved / learned / noticed:

_____

_____

_____

_____

Questions / things I want to research:

_____

_____

_____

_____

God Shot:

_____

_____

_____

_____

JOHN 11

Things I loved / learned / noticed:

_____

_____

_____

_____

Questions / things I want to research:

_____

_____

_____

_____

God Shot:

_____

_____

_____

_____

"Whoever believes in me, though he die, yet shall he
live, and everyone who lives and believes in me shall
never die. Do you believe this?"—John 11:25–26

LUKE 18

Things I loved / learned / noticed:

_____

_____

_____

_____

Questions / things I want to research:

_____

_____

_____

_____

God Shot:

_____

_____

_____

_____

In this life there will be losses, but Jesus promises
that what we gain for following Him will
always trump what we lose.

DATE

MATTHEW 19; MARK 10

Things I loved / learned / noticed:

_____

_____

_____

_____

Questions / things I want to research:

_____

_____

_____

_____

God Shot:

_____

_____

_____

_____

We all fall short of Jesus's teachings,
but He paid for our sins and took our shame.

MATTHEW 20–21

Things I loved / learned / noticed:

_____

_____

_____

_____

Questions / things I want to research:

_____

_____

_____

_____

God Shot:

_____

_____

_____

_____

LUKE 19

Things I loved / learned / noticed:

_____

_____

_____

_____

Questions / things I want to research:

_____

_____

_____

_____

God Shot:

_____

_____

_____

_____

"The Son of Man came to seek
and to save the lost."—Luke 19:10

MARK 11; JOHN 12

Things I loved / learned / noticed:

_____

_____

_____

_____

Questions / things I want to research:

_____

_____

_____

_____

God Shot:

_____

_____

_____

_____

We can't fix ourselves. We _must_ have the perfect
sacrifice—Jesus—to pay our sin debt.

DATE

MATTHEW 22; MARK 12

Things I loved / learned / noticed:

_____

_____

_____

_____

Questions / things I want to research:

_____

_____

_____

_____

God Shot:

_____

_____

_____

_____

The world ignores those who have nothing to offer,
but Jesus is drawn to the poor and the sinners.

MATTHEW 23; LUKE 20–21

Things I loved / learned / noticed:

_____

_____

_____

_____

Questions / things I want to research:

_____

_____

_____

_____

God Shot:

_____

_____

_____

_____

Whatever darkness comes our way
is no threat to God's light.

DATE

MARK 13

Things I loved / learned / noticed:

_____

_____

_____

_____

Questions / things I want to research:

_____

_____

_____

_____

God Shot:

_____

_____

_____

_____

Pray: Father, help me to share the gospel with others. You have given me life—eternal life—and I want the whole world to know Your love.

MATTHEW 24

Things I loved / learned / noticed:

_____

_____

_____

_____

Questions / things I want to research:

_____

_____

_____

_____

God Shot:

_____

_____

_____

_____

"Be ready, for the Son of Man is coming at an hour
you do not expect."—Matthew 24:44

MATTHEW 25

Things I loved / learned / noticed:

_____

_____

_____

_____

Questions / things I want to research:

_____

_____

_____

_____

God Shot:

_____

_____

_____

_____

Ultimately, we're responsible for how we use the time
and money and gifts God has entrusted us with.

MATTHEW 26; MARK 14

Things I loved / learned / noticed:

_____

_____

_____

_____

Questions / things I want to research:

_____

_____

_____

_____

God Shot:

_____

_____

_____

_____

By Jesus's blood our sins are covered.
By His death our lives are spared.

LUKE 22; JOHN 13

Things I loved / learned / noticed:

_____

_____

_____

_____

Questions / things I want to research:

_____

_____

_____

_____

God Shot:

_____

_____

_____

_____

JOHN 14–17

Things I loved / learned / noticed:

_____

_____

_____

_____

Questions / things I want to research:

_____

_____

_____

_____

God Shot:

_____

_____

_____

_____

Pray: Father, thank You for sending the Holy Spirit to dwell in Your people. Help me to discern and obey His voice and receive His encouragement.

MATTHEW 27; MARK 15

Things I loved / learned / noticed:

_____

_____

_____

_____

Questions / things I want to research:

_____

_____

_____

_____

God Shot:

_____

_____

_____

_____

Worldly sorrow is different from repentance and godly sorrow.

LUKE 23; JOHN 18–19

Things I loved / learned / noticed:

_____

_____

_____

_____

Questions / things I want to research:

_____

_____

_____

_____

God Shot:

_____

_____

_____

_____

"Jesus, calling out with a loud voice, said, 'Father, into your hands I commit my spirit!' And having said this he breathed his last."—Luke 23:46

MATTHEW 28; MARK 16

Things I loved / learned / noticed:

_____

_____

_____

_____

Questions / things I want to research:

_____

_____

_____

_____

God Shot:

_____

_____

_____

_____

Jesus has always gone to the rejected, the
outcasts, those considered "less than."

LUKE 24; JOHN 20–21

Things I loved / learned / noticed:

_____

_____

_____

_____

Questions / things I want to research:

_____

_____

_____

_____

God Shot:

_____

_____

_____

_____

"Blessed are those who have not seen and
yet have believed."—John 20:29

ACTS 1–3

Things I loved / learned / noticed:

_____

_____

_____

_____

Questions / things I want to research:

_____

_____

_____

_____

God Shot:

_____

_____

_____

_____

God doesn't grow impatient with us when we misunderstand.
He has the best ideas and the kindest heart.

ACTS 4–6

Things I loved / learned / noticed:

_____

_____

_____

_____

Questions / things I want to research:

_____

_____

_____

_____

God Shot:

_____

_____

_____

_____

Saving power isn't in the word _Jesus_;
it's in the person of Jesus.

DATE

ACTS 7–8

Things I loved / learned / noticed:

_____

_____

_____

_____

Questions / things I want to research:

_____

_____

_____

_____

God Shot:

_____

_____

_____

_____

What the enemy means for evil,
God uses for good.

ACTS 9–10

Things I loved / learned / noticed:

_____

_____

_____

_____

Questions / things I want to research:

_____

_____

_____

_____

God Shot:

_____

_____

_____

_____

"Peter opened his mouth and said: 'Truly I understand that God shows no partiality, but in every nation anyone who fears him and does what is right is acceptable to him.'"—Acts 10:34–35

ACTS 11–12

Things I loved / learned / noticed:

_____

_____

_____

_____

Questions / things I want to research:

_____

_____

_____

_____

God Shot:

_____

_____

_____

_____

God's the one who initiates our repentance.
What an incredible gift.

ACTS 13–14

Things I loved / learned / noticed:

_____

_____

_____

_____

Questions / things I want to research:

_____

_____

_____

_____

God Shot:

_____

_____

_____

_____

"The word of the Lord was spreading
throughout the whole region."—Acts 13:49

JAMES 1–5

Things I loved / learned / noticed:

_____

_____

_____

_____

Questions / things I want to research:

_____

_____

_____

_____

God Shot:

_____

_____

_____

_____

Pray: Father, help me to take my gaze off
myself and put it back on You.

ACTS 15–16

Things I loved / learned / noticed:

_____

_____

_____

_____

Questions / things I want to research:

_____

_____

_____

_____

God Shot:

_____

_____

_____

_____

"God, who knows the heart, bore witness to them, by giving
them the Holy Spirit just as he did to us."—Acts 15:8

GALATIANS 1–3

Things I loved / learned / noticed:

_____

_____

_____

_____

Questions / things I want to research:

_____

_____

_____

_____

God Shot:

_____

_____

_____

_____

Because of Christ, the door to God's kingdom is open to everyone.
And because of the Spirit, we're united across our differences.

GALATIANS 4–6

Things I loved / learned / noticed:

_____

_____

_____

_____

Questions / things I want to research:

_____

_____

_____

_____

God Shot:

_____

_____

_____

_____

The Spirit lives within us, and the one thing
He wants to do is magnify God.

ACTS 17

Things I loved / learned / noticed:

_____

_____

_____

_____

Questions / things I want to research:

_____

_____

_____

_____

God Shot:

_____

_____

_____

_____

1 THESSALONIANS 1–5;
2 THESSALONIANS 1–3

Things I loved / learned / noticed:

_____

_____

_____

_____

Questions / things I want to research:

_____

_____

_____

_____

God Shot:

_____

_____

_____

Pray: Father, thank You that it's You who does the good works
You desire through me. Keep making me more like You and
filling me up with Your faith and love to share with others.

ACTS 18–19

Things I loved / learned / noticed:

_____

_____

_____

_____

Questions / things I want to research:

_____

_____

_____

_____

God Shot:

_____

_____

_____

_____

God is always at work
on your behalf.

1 CORINTHIANS 1–4

Things I loved / learned / noticed:

_____

_____

_____

_____

Questions / things I want to research:

_____

_____

_____

_____

God Shot:

_____

_____

_____

_____

As God, the Spirit knows the mind of God.
As our Teacher, He helps us understand God's thoughts.

DATE

1 CORINTHIANS 5–8

Things I loved / learned / noticed:

_____

_____

_____

_____

Questions / things I want to research:

_____

_____

_____

_____

God Shot:

_____

_____

_____

_____

"You are not your own, for you were bought with a price.
So glorify God in your body."—1 Corinthians 6:19–20

1 CORINTHIANS 9–11

Things I loved / learned / noticed:

_____

_____

_____

_____

Questions / things I want to research:

_____

_____

_____

_____

God Shot:

_____

_____

_____

_____

Whether our sins are subtle or drastic,
they represent self-idolatry.

1 CORINTHIANS 12–14

Things I loved / learned / noticed:

_____

_____

_____

_____

Questions / things I want to research:

_____

_____

_____

_____

God Shot:

_____

_____

_____

_____

God isn't building a one-dimensional kingdom where
we all look and act the same. He loves diversity.

1 CORINTHIANS 15–16

Things I loved / learned / noticed:

Questions / things I want to research:

God Shot:

"Be steadfast, immovable, always abounding in the work of the Lord,
knowing that in the Lord your labor is not in vain."—1 Corinthians 15:58

2 CORINTHIANS 1–4

Things I loved / learned / noticed:

_____

_____

_____

_____

Questions / things I want to research:

_____

_____

_____

_____

God Shot:

_____

_____

_____

_____

Those who carry Christ carry a light in them
that God shined into their hearts.

2 CORINTHIANS 5–9

Things I loved / learned / noticed:

_____

_____

_____

_____

Questions / things I want to research:

_____

_____

_____

_____

God Shot:

_____

_____

_____

_____

Pray: Jesus, teach me to be a minister
of reconciliation, pointing others to You.

2 CORINTHIANS 10–13

Things I loved / learned / noticed:

_____

_____

_____

_____

Questions / things I want to research:

_____

_____

_____

_____

God Shot:

_____

_____

_____

_____

ROMANS 1–3

Things I loved / learned / noticed:

_____

_____

_____

_____

Questions / things I want to research:

_____

_____

_____

_____

God Shot:

_____

_____

_____

_____

We're all under the curse of sin and need God's rescue.

DATE

ROMANS 4–7

Things I loved / learned / noticed:

Questions / things I want to research:

God Shot:

"God shows his love for us in that while we were still sinners, Christ died for us."—Romans 5:8

ROMANS 8–10

Things I loved / learned / noticed:

_____

_____

_____

_____

Questions / things I want to research:

_____

_____

_____

_____

God Shot:

_____

_____

_____

_____

God can give people the ears to hear the gospel,
so we must be the mouths to speak it.

ROMANS 11–13

Things I loved / learned / noticed:

_____

_____

_____

_____

Questions / things I want to research:

_____

_____

_____

_____

God Shot:

_____

_____

_____

_____

Our God is unsearchable. Yet in His generosity,
He makes Himself knowable.

ROMANS 14–16

Things I loved / learned / noticed:

_____

_____

_____

_____

Questions / things I want to research:

_____

_____

_____

_____

God Shot:

_____

_____

_____

_____

"Welcome one another as Christ has welcomed
you, for the glory of God."—Romans 15:7

ACTS 20–23

Things I loved / learned / noticed:

_____

_____

_____

_____

Questions / things I want to research:

_____

_____

_____

_____

God Shot:

_____

_____

_____

_____

God has infinite power
and an infinite attention span.

ACTS 24–26

Things I loved / learned / noticed:

_____

_____

_____

_____

Questions / things I want to research:

_____

_____

_____

_____

God Shot:

_____

_____

_____

_____

Pray: Father, direct my steps according to Your will. May I make decisions with my mind on eternity and my heart on Your glory.

ACTS 27–28

Things I loved / learned / noticed:

_____

_____

_____

_____

Questions / things I want to research:

_____

_____

_____

_____

God Shot:

_____

_____

_____

_____

God reaches across enemy lines to show mercy
and save those who oppose Him.

COLOSSIANS 1–4; PHILEMON 1

Things I loved / learned / noticed:

_____

_____

_____

_____

Questions / things I want to research:

_____

_____

_____

_____

God Shot:

_____

_____

_____

_____

As followers of Christ, may we treat everyone
with dignity and honor regardless of position.

EPHESIANS 1–6

Things I loved / learned / noticed:

_____

_____

_____

_____

Questions / things I want to research:

_____

_____

_____

_____

God Shot:

_____

_____

_____

_____

By being in God's Word today, you are strengthened for
another day of fighting the lies of the flesh and the enemy.

PHILIPPIANS 1–4

Things I loved / learned / noticed:

_____

_____

_____

_____

Questions / things I want to research:

_____

_____

_____

_____

God Shot:

_____

_____

_____

_____

"I am sure of this, that he who began a good work in you will bring it to completion at the day of Jesus Christ."—Philippians 1:6

1 TIMOTHY 1–6

Things I loved / learned / noticed:

_____

_____

_____

_____

Questions / things I want to research:

_____

_____

_____

_____

God Shot:

_____

_____

_____

_____

Pray: God, thank You that You know what I need.
Help me to set my hopes on You and not on money.

TITUS 1–3

Things I loved / learned / noticed:

Questions / things I want to research:

God Shot:

Where we are today is due entirely to the goodness
and loving kindness of God our Savior.

1 PETER 1–5

Things I loved / learned / noticed:

_____

_____

_____

_____

Questions / things I want to research:

_____

_____

_____

_____

God Shot:

_____

_____

_____

_____

"Keep loving one another earnestly,
since love covers a multitude of sins."—1 Peter 4:8

HEBREWS 1–6

Things I loved / learned / noticed:

Questions / things I want to research:

God Shot:

As believers, we can have full assurance of our hope
in Christ—a hope that anchors our souls!

HEBREWS 7–10

Things I loved / learned / noticed:

_____

_____

_____

_____

Questions / things I want to research:

_____

_____

_____

_____

God Shot:

_____

_____

_____

_____

Pray: Jesus, thank You for becoming the perfect sacrifice for my sin.
I'm so grateful that You've made a way for me to be with You forever.

HEBREWS 11–13

Things I loved / learned / noticed:

_____

_____

_____

_____

Questions / things I want to research:

_____

_____

_____

_____

God Shot:

_____

_____

_____

_____

Not only has God given us everything we need to do His
will, but He's also working in us to accomplish it.

2 TIMOTHY 1–4

Things I loved / learned / noticed:

Questions / things I want to research:

God Shot:

2 PETER 1–3; JUDE 1

Things I loved / learned / noticed:

_____

_____

_____

_____

Questions / things I want to research:

_____

_____

_____

_____

God Shot:

_____

_____

_____

_____

"May grace and peace be multiplied to you in the knowledge
of God and of Jesus our Lord."—2 Peter 1:2

1 JOHN 1–5

Things I loved / learned / noticed:

_____

_____

_____

_____

Questions / things I want to research:

_____

_____

_____

_____

God Shot:

_____

_____

_____

_____

Jesus didn't just set us free from the *penalty* of our sins;
He also set us free from the *bondage* to our sins.

2 JOHN 1; 3 JOHN 1

Things I loved / learned / noticed:

_____

_____

_____

_____

Questions / things I want to research:

_____

_____

_____

_____

God Shot:

_____

_____

_____

_____

God continually pours out grace to help heal wounds,
bridge gaps, and restore brokenness.

DATE _____

REVELATION 1–5

Things I loved / learned / noticed:

_____

_____

_____

_____

Questions / things I want to research:

_____

_____

_____

_____

God Shot:

_____

_____

_____

_____

"Blessed is the one who reads aloud the words
of this prophecy."—Revelation 1:3

REVELATION 6–11

Things I loved / learned / noticed:

Questions / things I want to research:

God Shot:

REVELATION 12–18

Things I loved / learned / noticed:

_____

_____

_____

_____

Questions / things I want to research:

_____

_____

_____

_____

God Shot:

_____

_____

_____

_____

Christ's victory over death and darkness
was His victory over all the enemies of light and life.

REVELATION 19–22

Things I loved / learned / noticed:

_____

_____

_____

_____

Questions / things I want to research:

_____

_____

_____

_____

God Shot:

_____

_____

_____

_____

People need to know that Jesus is really coming back,
judgment is really happening, and the free blessing of knowing
God and living with Him for eternity really awaits.

Additional Journaling Space

Additional Journaling Space

Additional Journaling Space

Additional Journaling Space

Additional Journaling Space

Books by Tara-Leigh Cobble

The Bible Recap

The Bible Recap Deluxe Edition

*The Bible Recap Study Guide: Daily Questions to Deepen Your
Understanding of the Entire Bible*